Your Body, Your Treasure

By Sandra Orellana
Illustrated by Nicolas Finol

Balboa Press books may be ordered through booksellers or by contacting:

Balboa Press
A Division of Hay House
1663 Liberty Drive
Bloomington, IN 47403
www.balboapress.com
1 (877) 407-4847

ISBN: 978-1-9822-3241-2 (sc)
ISBN: 978-1-9822-3242-9 (e)

Library of Congress Control Number: 2019911399

Print information available on the last page.

Balboa Press rev. date: 12/09/2019

BALBOA
PRESS
A DIVISION OF HAY HOUSE

Dedicated to my
daughter, Fabiana.

May you choose to be you, and enjoy every minute of it. May you always walk on the path of self-love and shine your light unconditionally. Thank you for existing.

Dear Mom:

Receive this book as a gift from my heart to yours. My wish is that it assists you as you walk by your daughter in her wondrous journey of self-discovery. I honor you for choosing to be led by boundless love and unconditional support.

We are in this together,

Sandra Orellana

To my precious
daughter,

My sweet, sweet girl,
  welcome to these pages.

Here are some secrets
I want to share with you

That women have passed down
to their daughters for ages.

When you,
infinite soul,
    were born into
this planet

You received a
    precious gift,
One you are blessed
    to inhabit.

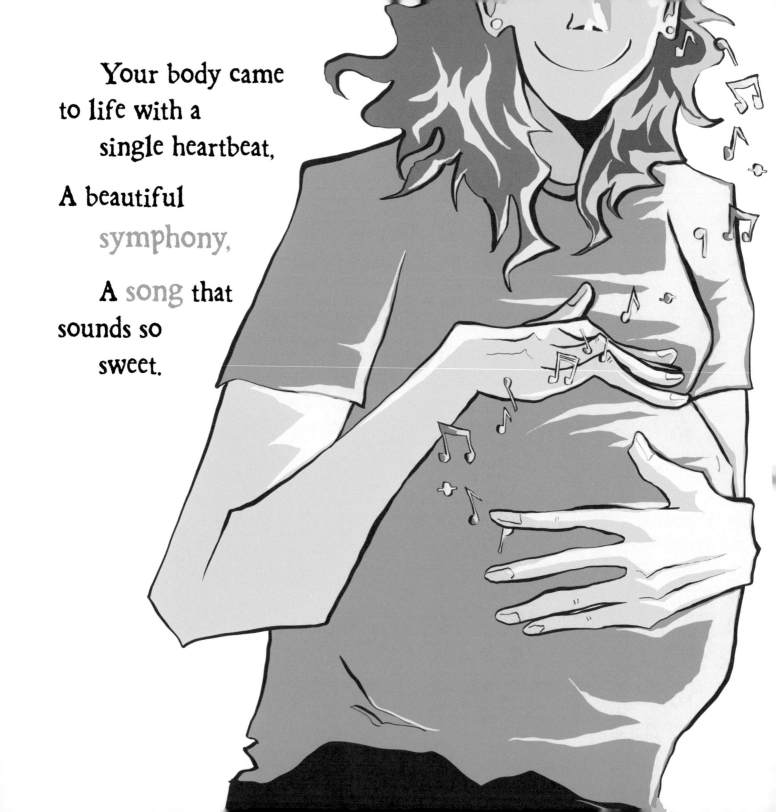

Your body came
to life with a
single heartbeat,

A beautiful
symphony,

A song that
sounds so
sweet.

You became free to discover
your body's many wonders.

As you enjoy
the journey,

Your relationship
with yourself

grows stronger.

Your body was designed to
move, grow, create, and feel.

It will change before your eyes,
It will hurt, it will heal.

You, my darling,
are the real deal.

Like a flower, that
    comes from a seed,
You must get all the
    nutrients you need.
Water, food,
    light, and love.

Respect is also
important,

And it begins
    as an
    inside job.

Your body, my dear,
   Is such a valuable treasure,

I hope this remains clear,

As you embark in the journey of
   following your pleasure.

If anyone is ever
    to touch you
In ways that
    don't feel right,

Please let me know,
I am here for you,
    We won't let anyone
dim your light.

And if you ever feel rejected,
    Remember you are safe and unaffected
        As long as your body and soul feel connected.

You see, my darling,

There is a bright light
    within you that always
guides your way.

Close your eyes,
feel your heart,
    and allow your
soul to play.

Your body was
    not the only gift
you received.

You were given
    incredible talents
and skills.

Accept them and
    share them,
that is all you need.

Being yourself
    is a wonderful thrill.

Your gifts make
    you YOU,
And lead the way to
    fulfill your
biggest dream.

To yourself be true,
    And remember I am
always on your team.

Sometimes, people will
    try to bring you down.

Threatened
    by your light,
they will try to
    steal your crown.

Whenever this happens,
   Focus on this thought:

You are beautiful and
   perfect exactly as you are.

Don't forget that,
   it will take you very far.

And as your body
changes and grows,

Feel how the love
inside of you
unconditionally
flows.

Let joy be your guide.
And allow your
worries to slide.

Dance, sing,
be silly, and smile.
Do the things that
make you happy,

Please do try them
for a while.

You are here
   to love yourself.

   All you
      need to do
   is BE.

Love who you are.
Don't forget
you're a star.

And never
fail to see,

You are
unconditionally
loved
and
supported
by me.

With love,

_____

Mom.

Acknowledgements:

Thank you, Noah Rosenberg, for reminding me how generosity unleashes magic. May we shed light on juvenile diabetes so that it ceases to be part of our future.

I am forever grateful to anyone who has ever been kind to me, especially to those who have inspired me to BE.

Sandra Orellana is an open-hearted mother of two, passionate about awakening self-acceptance and unconditional love wherever she goes. Sandra's background is in psychology, specialized in alternative healing techniques and social work. She co-creates healing/empowering circles with the purpose of learning and practicing protocols that align individuals with their most truthful and authentic power. Sandra strives to share art from her heart.

@raw__sandra

www.rawsandra.com

Printed in the United States
By Bookmasters